BEING A GOVERNOR

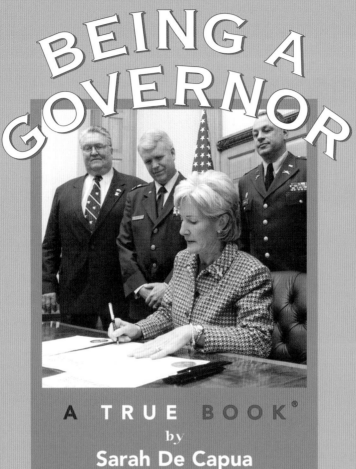

A TRUE BOOK®

by
Sarah De Capua

Children's Press®
A Division of Scholastic Inc.

New York Toronto London Auckland Sydney
Mexico City New Delhi Hong Kong
Danbury, Connecticut

Reading Consultant
Jeanne Clidas, Ph.D.
*National Reading Consultant
and Professor of Reading,
SUNY Brockport*

Content Consultant
Jonathan Riehl, J.D.
*Graduate Instructor,
Communication Studies
University of North Carolina,
Chapel Hill*

A governor visiting
with a student

Library of Congress Cataloging-in-Publication Data

De Capua, Sarah.
    Being a governor / by Sarah De Capua.
        p. cm. — (A true book)
    Summary: Describes the role of a state governor, who is qualified to
become governor, how one becomes governor, and how a typical day in
the life of a governor might unfold.
    Includes bibliographical references and index.
    ISBN 0-516-22797-1 (lib. bdg.)   0-516-27939-4 (pbk.)
1. Governors—United States—Juvenile literature. 2. Governors—
Juvenile literature. [1. Governors. 2. State government. 3. Occupations.]
I. Title. II. Series.
JK2447.D43 2003
352.23'213'0973—dc22   2003012514

6 7 8 9 10 R 13 12 11 10 09 08   62

Contents

A governor giving a speech to the state legislature

What Is a Governor?

You probably know that the president is the leader of the United States. Do you know who leads the state you live in? Whether you live in Maine or Hawaii, Illinois, or Alaska, your state is led by a governor. The governments of all the states were set up this way.

Each state has three branches of government: a legislative branch, a judicial branch, and an executive branch. This system is similar to that of the federal government. Each branch has its own duties. Power is divided among the three branches so that no branch can get too powerful.

The legislative branch, or state **legislature**, makes the state's laws. It also decides

The governor (at podium) and the state legislature work together to create laws.

how the state will spend state money. It is made up of law-makers who have been elected by the people of the state.

The judicial branch is made up of judges and their courts. When people have been accused of breaking the law, judges hear their cases. Judges may also help decide on the punishment to be given.

The executive branch carries out the state's laws and works to ensure that they are fair. The head of the executive branch is the governor. He or she works with other members of the executive branch.

A newly elected governor introduces some of the members of his staff.

A governor being sworn in to office

Governors are elected by the voters in their state. Most state governors serve a four-year **term**. In New Hampshire and Vermont, a governor's term lasts for two years. In some states, there is no limit on how many terms in a row a governor may be elected to serve. In others, governors can serve only two terms in a row. In Virginia, a governor may not serve **consecutive** terms—he or she is limited to one term at a time.

A governor's job is to provide leadership. He or she makes decisions regarding the day-to-day problems that exist in the state. Governors oversee many state departments and agencies. These include departments of health and human services and

After a tornado struck her state, this governor (at left) went to the site to see how she could best help the victims.

departments of transportation. These and other departments have many responsibilities. They exist to help the people of a state. The workers in these departments all have one boss— the governor!

Who Can Be a Governor?

Every state has a constitution. A constitution is a written document containing the **principles** by which each state is governed. State constitutions set the rules for who can become governor. These rules vary from state to state.

A candidate for governor of New Mexico greets a voter.

Usually, states require that a candidate for governor be a U.S. citizen. Someone who was born in the United States is a U.S. citizen. A person who was born in another country but has become **naturalized** is also a U.S. citizen.

Each state also has its own age requirement for becoming governor. Most state constitutions

Candidates for governor of Florida pose for the cameras before a debate.

say that the youngest a governor can be is thirty years old.

Finally, anyone wanting to be governor of a state must live in that state for a certain period of time before the **election**. In most states, the length of time is about five years. However, the required number of years may be as many as ten.

The job of governor is open to both men and women and to people of all ethnic and

The Honolulu Advertiser

LINGLE WINS

GOP defies history and takes control of Congress

KEY RESULTS

religious backgrounds. As long as a person meets the **qualifications** listed in the state constitution, he or she can become a **candidate** for governor of that state.

States' Rules

Here are some examples of what various states require of a person who wishes to run for governor:

Georgia: A candidate must be a U.S. citizen for at least five years. He or she must live in the state for six years before the election. The candidate must be at least thirty years old.

Maine: A candidate must be a U.S. citizen for fifteen years. He or she must live in Maine for at least five years before the election. The candidate must be at least thirty years old.

Missouri: A candidate must be a U.S. citizen for at least fifteen years. He or she must live in Missouri for ten years prior to the election. The candidate must be at least thirty years old.

Montana: A candidate must be a U.S. citizen. He or she must live in Montana for at least two years before the election. The candidate must be at least twenty-five years old.

Governors from the states of Georgia (opposite top), Maine (opposite bottom), Missouri (above), and Montana (left)

Governor's Role

The most important parts of a governor's job are providing leadership and carrying out the laws that govern the people of his or her state. The laws of a particular state are made by that state's legislature.

Proposed laws, called bills, become official laws when the

After signing a bill into law, a governor (at right) shakes hands with supporters of the bill.

governor signs them. A governor may also veto a bill, or refuse to sign it into law. State legislatures, however, have the power to override the governor's veto.

To do this, a certain number of state legislators (usually two-thirds) must vote to override the governor's veto. If this happens, the bill becomes law even without the governor's signature.

When the legislature meets each year, the governor attends the first session and makes a speech. This speech is called the State of the State Address. In the speech, the governor details problems the state is facing and tells the legislature

A governor giving his State of the State Address

about the ideas he or she has for fixing those problems.

After the legislature has met for a few weeks, the governor sends a state budget to the legislature. A budget is a plan for how state money will be earned and spent. The members of the legislature vote on whether to pass the budget. When the budget is approved by the legislature, it goes back

A governor discusses the state budget with the state legislature.

to the governor. As with most new state laws, the budget becomes official when the governor signs it.

As bills are discussed in the legislature, the governor meets

A governor (at left) talks with a legislator about a bill.

with lawmakers. The meetings are held to discuss how close the bills are to being passed. The governor meets with lawmakers who support bills that the governor supports or are against bills that the governor is against. Together, they plan the best way to get these bills passed or defeated.

The governor also meets with people who do not support the governor's position on certain bills. This is a chance to convince these lawmakers to vote the way the governor wants. It is also a chance to compromise, or to make changes that everyone can agree to. Sometimes governors appear before committees in the

A governor appearing before a legislative committee to argue in favor of a bill

legislature to argue in support of or against a bill.

Another important role of a governor is to convince the voters of a state that he or she is doing a good job. Governors stay in touch with state voters in order to gain or keep their support. Some of the ways governors reach out to voters are through press conferences, speeches, and appearances at public events.

This governor (at left) is talking with voters to find out what their concerns are.

Lieutenant Governors

The lieutenant governor of a state is like the vice president of the United States. He or she must always be ready to take over if anything happens to the governor.

In some states, the governor and lieutenant governor are elected together. This means they are both from the same **political party**.

A lieutenant governor from Wisconsin

In other states, they are elected separately. This means the governor could be from one political party and the lieutenant governor could be from another.

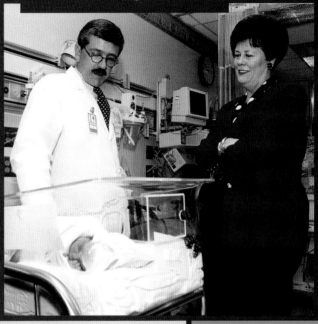

A Florida lieutenant governor

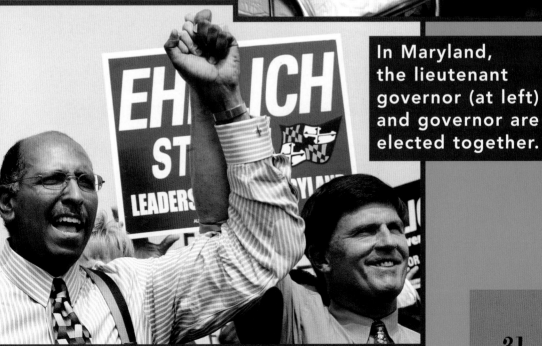

In Maryland, the lieutenant governor (at left) and governor are elected together.

A Governor's Day

A day in the life of a state governor is a busy one. Governors travel often. Their many varied responsibilities mean no two days are exactly alike. Here is an example of the type of day a governor might have.

The governor awakes at about 6 A.M. in the governor's

The Nevada governor's mansion

mansion. The governor's mansion is a home built especially for the governor and his or her family. Every state has one.

By 8 A.M., it is time to leave for the governor's office. The governor is usually driven to and from the statehouse, where the governor's office and the state legislature are located. The governor rides in a car that is specially built for extra protection. When governors travel long distances, they ride in private planes.

On the way from place to place, the governor reads reports, answers E-mails, or

A governor (at right) traveling to an event on a private plane

types letters. He or she may review a speech that is about to be delivered.

When the governor arrives
at his or her office, meetings
with different people may
take place. Sometimes, the

A governor (at right) holds
a meeting with a former
governor of his state.

A governor's day may include appearances at special events, such as this ribbon-cutting ceremony for a new learning center at an elementary school.

governor must appear at an event, such as a ground-breaking ceremony for a new public building. Afterward,

Governors often hold press conferences and interviews.

television or newspaper reporters may be expecting to interview the governor.

When the governor returns to the office, more meetings may take place. He or she may have lunch with a state legislator to discuss an important issue. During the afternoon, the governor may speak before the state legislature.

The governor then may return to his or her office for a meeting with state citizens who want to bring a problem or issue to the governor's

A governor catching up on paperwork in his office

attention. After the meeting, the governor may check for voice mail or E-mail, or make and return telephone calls.

At about 6 P.M., the governor is driven home. On the way, he or she might read newspapers or check the news online.

When the governor returns to the mansion, the day may not be over yet. There may be a dinner party at the governor's mansion that night. Some of these events are called fundraisers. Fundraisers are held for the purpose of raising money. For example, the governor might be raising money for his or her political party. The money will help the party get more members elected to public office.

Finally, at around 10 or 11 P.M.—and sometimes later—the governor's work is finished. It has been a busy day.

Do you think you could do a governor's job?

A governor
at home
with his dog

To Find Out More

Here are some additional resources to help you learn more about governors and state government:

Books

De Capua, Sarah. **Becoming a Citizen.** Children's Press, 2002.

De Capua, Sarah. **Making a Law.** Children's Press, 2004.

De Capua, Sarah. **Running for Public Office.** Children's Press, 2002.

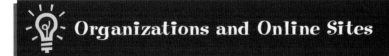

Organizations and Online Sites

National Governors Association

http://www.nga.org

Hall of States
444 N. Capitol Street
Washington, DC 20001

This site contains news and information about issues relating to each state.

U.S. Governors

http://www.ourcampaigns. com

Do you know the name of the governor of your state? Check out this site to find names and photographs of the governors of all fifty states.

Your State's Homepage

http://www.state.(type your state's two-letter zip code abbreviation here).us

If you type the above address into your web browser, substituting your state's two-letter zip code (for example AL, AR, CT, IL, ME, RI, WA, etc.) you'll find your state's homepage. Click on it to find all kinds of information and kids' pages about how your state's government works.

Important Words

candidate person running for public office

consecutive happening or following one after another

election process of choosing someone or deciding something by voting

legislature group of people who have the power to make or change laws for a country or state

naturalized having gone through the process of earning citizenship after being born in another country

political party organized group of people with similar beliefs who try to win elections

principles basic rules that govern people's behavior

qualifications abilities that allow one to do a job or carry out an office

term definite or limited period of time

Index

Meet the Author

Sarah De Capua works as an editor and author of children's books. As the author of many nonfiction works, she enjoys educating children through her books. Other titles she has written in the True Books series include *Becoming a Citizen, How People Immigrate, Making a Law, Paying Taxes, Running for Public Office, Serving on a Jury,* and *Voting.*

Born and raised in Connecticut, Ms. De Capua currently resides in Colorado.